D0471602

J

DALY CITY PUBLIC LIBRARY
DALY CITY, CALIFORNIA

Isaac Asimov's

21st Century

Library of the
Universe

Near and Far

The Milky Way and Other Galaxies

BY ISAAC ASIMOV
WITH REVISIONS AND UPDATING BY RICHARD HANTULA

Gareth Stevens Publishing
A WORLD ALMANAC EDUCATION GROUP COMPANY

J

J
J523.1/2
ASI

Please visit our web site at: www.garethstevens.com
For a free color catalog describing Gareth Stevens Publishing's list of high-quality
books and multimedia programs, call 1-800-542-2595 (USA) or 1-800-387-3178 (Canada).
Gareth Stevens Publishing's fax: (414) 332-3567.

The reproduction rights to all photographs and illustrations in this book are controlled by the individuals
or institutions credited on page 32 and may not be reproduced without their permission.

Library of Congress Cataloging-in-Publication Data

Asimov, Isaac.
    The Milky Way and other galaxies / by Isaac Asimov; with revisions and updating by Richard Hantula.
       p. cm. — (Isaac Asimov's 21st century library of the universe. Near and far)
    Includes bibliographical references and index.
    ISBN 0-8368-3968-4 (lib. bdg.)
    1. Galaxies—Juvenile literature. 2. Milky Way—Juvenile literature. I. Hantula, Richard.
  II. Asimov, Isaac. Our vast home. III. Title.
  QB857.3.A85   2005
  523.1'12—dc22   2004058313

This edition first published in 2005 by
Gareth Stevens Publishing
A WRC Media Company
330 West Olive Street, Suite 100
Milwaukee, WI 53212 USA

Revised and updated edition © 2005 by Gareth Stevens, Inc. Original edition published in 1988
by Gareth Stevens, Inc. under the title *Our Milky Way and Other Galaxies*. Second edition
published in 1995 by Gareth Stevens, Inc. under the title *Our Vast Home: The Milky Way
and Other Galaxies*. Text © 2005 by Nightfall, Inc. End matter and revisions © 2005
by Gareth Stevens, Inc.

Series editor: Mark J. Sachner
Cover design and layout adaptation: Melissa Valuch
Picture research: Kathy Keller
Additional picture research: Diane Laska-Swanke
Artwork commissioning: Kathy Keller and Laurie Shock
Production director: Jessica Morris

The editors at Gareth Stevens Publishing have selected science author Richard Hantula to bring
this classic series of young people's information books up to date. Richard Hantula has written
and edited books and articles on science and technology for more than two decades. He was
the senior U.S. editor for the *Macmillan Encyclopedia of Science*.

In addition to Hantula's contribution to this most recent edition, the editors would like to
acknowledge the participation of two noted science authors, Greg Walz-Chojnacki and
Francis Reddy, as contributors to earlier editions of this work.

All rights to this edition reserved to Gareth Stevens, Inc. No part of this book may be reproduced,
stored in a retrieval system, or transmitted in any form or by any means, electronic, mechanical,
photocopying, recording, or otherwise, without the prior written permission of the publisher except
for the inclusion of brief quotations in an acknowledged review.

Printed in the United States of America

1 2 3 4 5 6 7 8 9 09 08 07 06 05

Contents

The Milky Way and Other Galaxies

We live in an enormously large place – the Universe. It's only natural that we would want to understand this place, so scientists and engineers have developed instruments and spacecraft that have told us far more about the Universe than we could possibly imagine.

We have seen planets up close, and spacecraft have even landed on some. We have learned about quasars and pulsars, supernovas and colliding galaxies, and black holes and dark matter. We have gathered amazing data about how the Universe may have come into being and how it may end. Nothing could be more astonishing.

Looking toward the sky with unaided eyes, we can see thousands of stars. With telescopes, we can see billions more. Our Sun is just one star in all these billions. Our group of stars is called the Milky Way. We have learned of many other groups of stars, called galaxies, existing in our vast Universe. In this book, you will be given a glimpse of our Galaxy and the billions of galaxies beyond.

Our Home: The Milky Way

After dark, away from city lights, look up at the faint, foggy band crossing the sky. This band is called the Milky Way.

After the invention of the telescope in the early seventeenth century, astronomers discovered that the Milky Way is made up of billions of very faint stars.

Astronomers observing the sky in the late eighteenth century saw that the stars exist in a huge collection shaped like a pancake. They named this collection of stars *galaxy*, from the Greek word for "milk."

Astronomers first thought our Sun must be located near the center of our Galaxy. But later they found that the center was about 26,000 light-years away from our Solar System.

A light-year is the distance traveled by light in one year — nearly 6 trillion miles or 9.5 trillion kilometers. At that speed, light travels from the Sun to Earth in about eight minutes. If you could travel at the speed of light, you could go around the world 7.5 times in one second!

Left: This photograph of the Milky Way was taken in the desert of Arizona.

Visible and Invisible

Our Galaxy is well over 100,000 light-years wide. It is made up of a central ball of older stars and a flat outer disk of gas, dust, and younger stars. The Galaxy thus looks like it has a bulge in the center. The disk is surrounded by a "halo" made up of separate stars and ball-shaped groups of stars called globular clusters.

Our Sun lies not in the central bulge but in the outer disk. When we look at the Milky Way in the sky, the Galaxy's center does not seem bright at all, even though it has lots of stars. This is because dust clouds hide the center from our view.

But the center is not the only part of the Galaxy that we cannot see. Even scientists, with their powerful instruments, can "see" only a small part of the matter that makes up the Milky Way. They believe that most of the material in our Galaxy – and in the other galaxies of the Universe – is a mysterious substance called dark matter. This dark matter does not give off light or other radiation and so is impossible to observe directly. Scientists who have studied the gravitational effects of dark matter think that in our Galaxy it extends far beyond the parts that can be seen.

Above: A false-color photo showing a portion of the Milky Way Galaxy as mapped by an optical viewing device. This is an expanded version of the view that appears on the next page in the third row from the bottom.

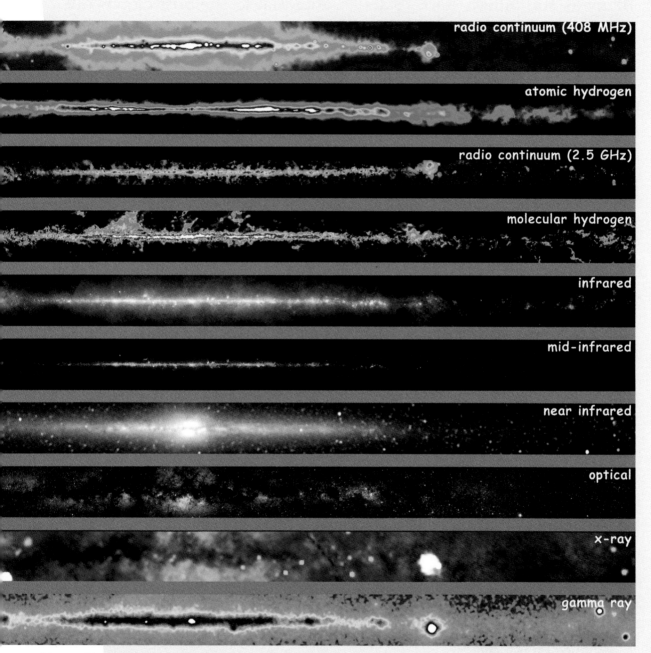

radio continuum (408 MHz)

atomic hydrogen

radio continuum (2.5 GHz)

molecular hydrogen

infrared

mid-infrared

near infrared

optical

x-ray

gamma ray

Above: Many details of the Milky Way cannot be seen when you look at the sky with your eyes or with an ordinary telescope. These false-color maps show a part of the sky containing the Milky Way Galaxy as it appears when viewed with special instruments that respond to different kinds of electromagnetic radiation, such as light, or "optical" radiation *(third from bottom)*; gamma rays *(bottom)*; and various kinds of radio waves *(top)*.

Stages of the Stars

In our Galaxy, there may be as many as 400 billion stars! Stars form out of large clouds of dust and gas. With so many stars in our Galaxy, there are different kinds of stars at different stages of their lives. Our Sun formed nearly five billion years ago. Other stars are forming today. And since stars don't live forever, many stars are dying at this very moment. The biggest ones eventually explode and add more material to the dust clouds out of which new stars form. Very massive stars exist only a few million years before exploding as supernovas. Our own Sun will live for billions of years and then turn into a red giant star. After that, it will come to a quiet end as it shrinks into a white dwarf star and then cools off to form a black dwarf.

Above: A supernova *(center)* in the Large Magellanic Cloud, a "mini-galaxy" that is a satellite, or companion, of our Galaxy.

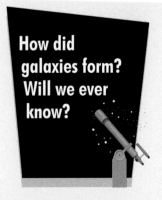

How did galaxies form? Will we ever know?

Astronomers think that when the Universe formed, it was a small object with all its mass evenly spread out. How did that mass break up into clumps to form the galaxies? Some scientists suggest that clumps developed because of the presence of a special sort of dark matter called cold dark matter, which could form clumps more readily than could other types of matter. Other scientists have other ideas, but no one really knows for certain.

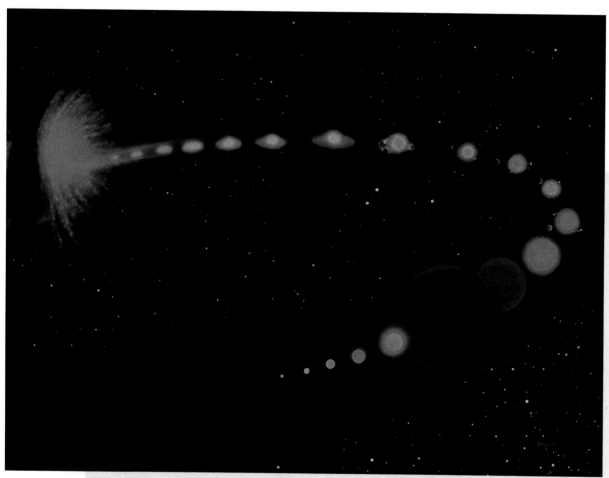

Above: Stages in the life of a star like our Sun. From a cloud of gas and dust *(far left)* there form a star and surrounding disk *(rear, center)*, which develop into a solar system like our own *(rear, right)*. After billions of years, the star expands, becoming a red giant *(front, right)*, and then collapses into a white dwarf *(front, left)*.

Star Groups

The cloud of dust and gas that became our Sun formed only a single star, plus its planets. But such clouds often form more than one star.

Binary stars — stars that circle each other — are quite common. Some stars consist of two pairs, or even three. In fact, stars begin their lives in large groups, and the sky holds many collections of young stars. Then there are the globular clusters that tend to be found in the outlying regions of the Galaxy. These balls — made up of thousands or even millions of older stars — are quite closely packed. In fact, the entire Galaxy, which contains hundreds of billions of stars, probably started as a vast cloud of gas.

Right: The Pleiades star cluster, in the constellation Taurus, formed from an enormous cloud of gas and dust. This cluster is so young that some of the leftover gas from the cloud is still visible.

Above: A small section of the incredibly closely packed center of the huge Omega Centauri globular star cluster, as viewed by the Hubble Space Telescope.

The Magellanic Clouds

The Milky Way is just one of more than 100 billion galaxies in the Universe. Some are larger than the Milky Way, but some are smaller. In the Southern Hemisphere, two dim clouds can be seen in the night sky that look as though they are pieces of the Milky Way that have broken loose. In fact, they are small irregularly shaped satellite galaxies of our Galaxy. They are called the Large Magellanic Cloud and the Small Magellanic Cloud — in honor of the Portuguese explorer Ferdinand Magellan, who was the first European to see them. The Large Magellanic Cloud is about 180,000 light-years from our Galaxy's center and contains perhaps 10 to 15 billion stars. The Small Magellanic Cloud, a bit farther away, has only a few billion stars.

Above: Visible to the naked eye south of the Equator is the Small Magellanic Cloud.

Is the Universe ruled by the dark side?

In the past, scientists thought most of the mass of a galaxy was located in its center. If this were true, then a star's rate of motion should drop off in a certain way the farther the star gets from the center. But when actually measured, the rate of motion doesn't drop off the way it should. There must be more mass in the outer regions than can be seen. Perhaps the "missing mass" is dark matter, but even that can't explain everything scientists have found. Research reported in 2003 suggested that ordinary matter accounts for only 4 percent of the Universe, and dark matter only 23 percent, with the rest represented by a mysterious "dark energy."

Above: People south of the Equator can also see the
Large Magellanic Cloud without instruments.
Astronomers have studied this galaxy to
gain insights into our own Galaxy.

The Andromeda Galaxy is the most distant object that can be seen with the naked eye. It lies nearly three million light-years away and is visible in dark country skies during autumn. Both the Andromeda Galaxy and our own Milky Way are called spiral galaxies, because they feature spiral arms winding through their disks.

Milky Way

Andromeda Galaxy

Right: A family portrait of the Local Group of galaxies. Most of its members are small, or "dwarf," galaxies. Several dwarf galaxies orbit the Milky Way as satellites. The majority of the galaxies in the Local Group are shaped like round or oval balls, others are irregular in shape, and only three are spiral galaxies.

The Local Group

In the 1920s, astronomers realized that a faint patch of light in the constellation Andromeda is actually a galaxy far outside our own. It is the Andromeda Galaxy, and it lies close to three million light-years from the Milky Way. The Andromeda Galaxy, the Milky Way, and more than three dozen other nearby galaxies make up what is known as the Local Group. The Local Group's members are all locked together with each other by gravity.

Most members of the Local Group are small, or dwarf, galaxies, some of which are satellites of the Andromeda Galaxy or the Milky Way. The satellite closest to the Milky Way is the Canis Major Dwarf, which is estimated to have only about a billion stars. It was discovered in 2003 and is named for the constellation, Canis Major, in which it is located. It is only about 42,000 light-years from the center of our Galaxy and is being torn apart by the Milky Way's gravitational pull.

Island universes — another name for galaxies?

In 1755 the German philosopher Immanuel Kant wondered about certain foggy patches in the sky. Kant thought these patches were distant collections of stars. He called them "island universes." Other astronomers of the time thought the foggy patches were just clouds of dust and gas fairly close to Earth. It took astronomers nearly two hundred more years to determine that Kant was right about the foggy patches being collections of stars. What Kant called island universes are now called galaxies.

A giant cluster of galaxies about 4.5 billion light-years from Earth. This picture is actually a map of the matter in and around the galaxies. The blue area shows where invisible dark matter is located, according to measurements and calculations made by astronomers.

Above: A 2004 image from the Hubble Space Telescope showing galaxies billions of light-years away.

Galaxies Galore

A cluster like the Local Group isn't so unusual. Like stars, galaxies tend to exist in clusters. Our Local Group is a rather small cluster of galaxies. Larger clusters exist, too. In the constellation Coma Berenices, there is a cluster that contains more than a thousand galaxies. This cluster is about 300 million light-years away. Nearer to us is a cluster of galaxies in the constellation Virgo that is made up of more than 2,000 galaxies. Other clusters with thousands of galaxies have also been discovered. Our own Galaxy, huge though it is, is only one of many billions of galaxies in our Universe. We haven't even begun to count them all!

Right: The Virgo cluster of galaxies. This is an irregular cluster, which means that it is not so tightly concentrated toward the cluster's center.

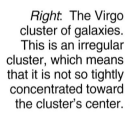

Clusters, superclusters, soapsuds!

Just as galaxies are grouped in clusters, galaxy clusters are grouped in superclusters. A supercluster may contain dozens or even hundreds of clusters. Superclusters are situated around enormous round regions of space called voids. These voids, which are more or less empty, may be as large as 100 million to 400 million light-years across. This means that superclusters are arranged in space in a way that looks something like bubbly foam or soapsuds!

The Spiral Milky Way

Not all galaxies are shaped the same. Many are elliptical, or oval-shaped. Others are spirals, with flat, round, swirly shapes. Still others are irregular in shape.

Our Milky Way is a spiral galaxy. It has several long, curved lines of stars, called spiral arms. These curve into the central part of the Galaxy. Astronomers trace the spiral arms by following the young, giant blue stars they contain. All the stars in the arms move around the center of the Galaxy. The Sun circles the center once every 220 million years. It is located in an arm called Orion. Other arms that scientists have identified include the Centaurus, Sagittarius, Perseus, and Cygnus arms.

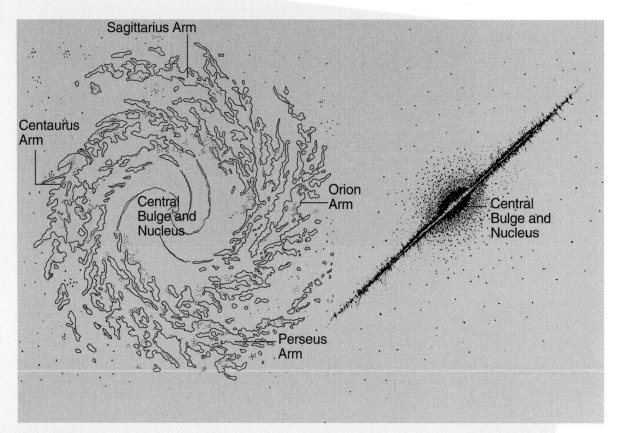

Above: Here is a closer look at the images on the opposite page, with some of the major parts of our Galaxy pointed out.

Above: Two views of the Milky Way Galaxy – at *left* is a face-on view, with the spirals whirling around the center; at *right* is a view from the side, with the spirals forming a disk intersected by the center. The center bulges with old stars, while the spiral arms contain many brightly shining new stars. Stars in the halo surrounding the main disk tend to be old.

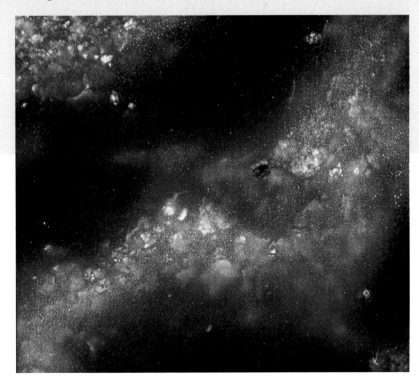

Right: Because our Solar System is on the inner edge of the Orion arm, we get a spectacular view of the neighboring arm — the Sagittarius arm, pictured.

The arms of some spiral galaxies begin at the ends of a long cloud of stars called a bar. The "barred spiral" galaxy shown here is located about 60 million light-years from Earth.

Above: Do you see why this spiral galaxy is called the Sombrero Galaxy?

Great Spiral Beauties

Our Milky Way is a wonderful sight. But, of course, we can only see it from the inside, so we don't get a good overall view of it. However, we can see other galaxies, and some of them have beautiful spiral shapes, especially if we happen to see them face-on. The spiral Andromeda Galaxy is at a slant, but the arms can still be seen. Only the edges of some spiral galaxies, like the Sombrero Galaxy, are visible. With these spirals, a line of dust clouds can usually be seen along the edge of the rim. Almost every spiral galaxy is beautiful in its own way.

Above: The M81 Galaxy is one of the most visible and familiar of the spiral galaxies. This computer-enhanced picture shows the younger stars in the arms as teal blue and the older stars of the disk as orange.

A spiral galaxy visible from Earth's Southern Hemisphere.

Spectacular Ellipticals

Many galaxies do not have spiral structures. They seem to be made up just of centers, without arms. Galaxies of this type whose outlines are oval are called elliptical galaxies. Many elliptical galaxies are rather small and dim, but some are giants.

Large clusters of galaxies often contain many ellipticals, and the largest ellipticals may have up to a hundred times as many stars as our Galaxy does!

Right: An example of a rare "polar-ring" galaxy, which features a ring of stars rotating around a central group of stars. Some astronomers think this odd galaxy, called NGC 4650A, was created by the collision of two galaxies long ago.

How many stars did you say?

The average spiral galaxy may have about 100,000,000,000 (one hundred billion) stars. Some giant elliptical galaxies have a hundred times that number. On the other hand, there are many dwarf galaxies with only one-tenth the average number, or even less.

Still, if we assume that one hundred billion stars per galaxy is the average and if we assume there are about a hundred billion galaxies, then the total number of stars in the Universe is about ten sextillion — that's 10 followed by twenty-one zeros!

Above: The elliptical galaxy Centaurus A is one of the brightest and largest of the known galaxies. Many scientists believe that the dark dust band running across the galaxy is a result of a collision with a spiral galaxy not too long ago.

Above: Galaxy NGC 2787 is shaped something like a lens. Such "lenticular" galaxies are flattish and either lack arms or (as in the case of NGC 2787) seem to reveal hints of "arms" that fail to show the beautiful structure seen in spiral galaxies.

Black Hole Centers

Some galaxies give off enormous amounts of energy from their center. Astronomers believe that this energy is released because of the presence of a colossal black hole. A black hole is an extremely tightly packed object whose gravity is so strong that not even light can escape from it. This means that it is impossible to see a black hole directly. The interaction of a massive black hole's powerful gravity with nearby matter, however, may release energy, such as light or other types of radiation, that makes it possible to detect the black hole's presence.

The giant elliptical galaxy called M87 was one of the first galaxies where astronomers found strong evidence for the existence of a "supermassive" black hole at the center. It had long been known that a mysterious jet of matter was shooting out from M87's center. In 1994 the Hubble Space Telescope revealed the existence of a whirling disk of hot gas at the center. A supermassive black hole was the only thing that could account for this disk's characteristics.

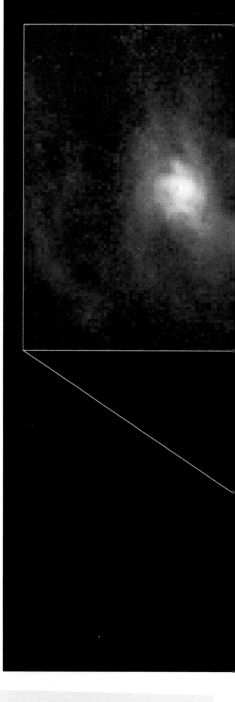

Very — make that incredibly — distant galaxies

There are galaxies that are very far — over a billion light-years — away. A few galaxies that are that far away have very active centers. Those centers blaze so brightly they can be seen even when the rest of the galaxy cannot be. At one time, astronomers detected certain dim stars they thought belonged to our own Galaxy. Imagine their surprise when they realized they were looking at the centers of incredibly distant galaxies. Those far-off active centers were named quasars. They are among the most distant known objects in the Universe!

Above: In 1994 the Hubble Space Telescope peered into the heart of the galaxy M87 and revealed that a swirling disk was connected with the jet of matter that shoots out from the galaxy's center. Scientists believed that only a black hole could account for this disk. The jet is visible at *upper right*. The disk itself is shown in the inset at *upper left*.

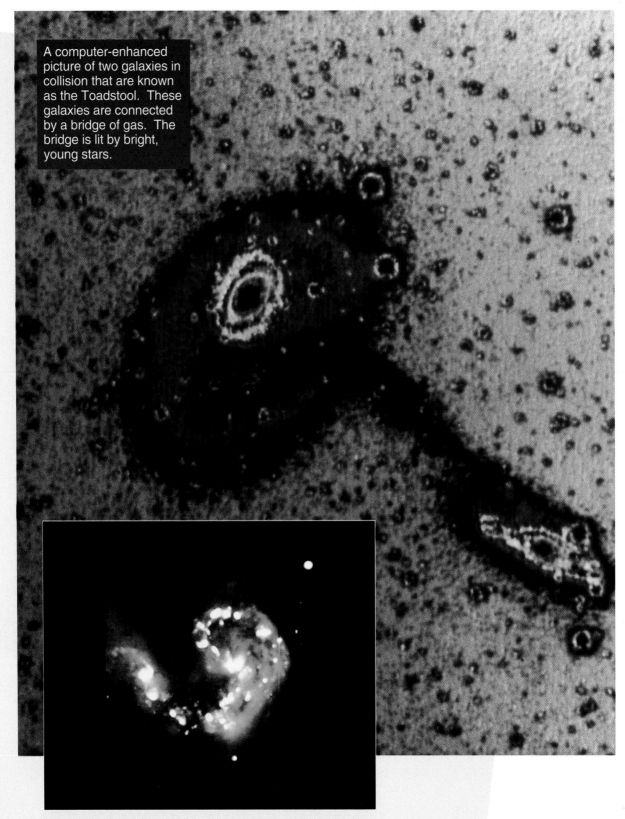

A computer-enhanced picture of two galaxies in collision that are known as the Toadstool. These galaxies are connected by a bridge of gas. The bridge is lit by bright, young stars.

Above: A dramatic collision between two galaxies forms what is called the Antennae, or the Rattail Galaxies. This encounter began hundreds of millions of years ago.

Cannibal Galaxies

It's a big Universe. In most cases, stars are so far apart that they pass each other harmlessly. But galaxies in clusters do move around. As a result, some galaxies collide with each other.

Colliding galaxies can have an effect on one another. The breaking up of dust clouds, for example, can produce a lot of radiation. And if galaxies collide head on, they sometimes remain together. In fact, the giant galaxies in some clusters may be as large as they are because they have swallowed others. Such giants are sometimes called "cannibal galaxies" for that reason.

We cannot be absolutely sure, but in a few billion years our Galaxy may collide with the Andromeda Galaxy. Who knows what the effects would be? For now, at least, we're safe in our corner of the Milky Way!

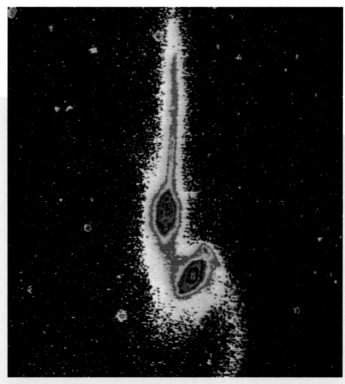

Above: This computer-enhanced picture shows streams of gas created by the interaction of two galaxies called the Mice.

Fact File: Constellations — Our Map of the Milky Way

When you look into the sky at the Milky Way, you see stars — thousands of them at once. Some of these stars stand out from the rest. For centuries, people have believed that certain stars form patterns or even pictures in the sky.

These patterns of stars are called constellations. Most constellations are named after gods and heroes from ancient Greek mythology, animals, scientific instruments, and various objects that were in common use long ago.

The stars that make up any one constellation are not actually close together. They just look that way from our viewpoint on Earth.

Constellations help us find stars, planets, and other objects in the sky. They are our map of the Milky Way.

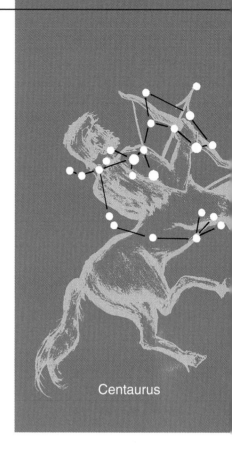

Centaurus

The Galaxy of Numbers

How big and far away are objects in the Universe? You probably know what a two-story school building looks like. If you have ever watched a baseball game, you can imagine 90 feet (27.5 meters) – the distance between each base. And you can probably figure out about how long 2 hours seems – or 24 hours, which makes 1 day.

But what if we say that light travels nearly 6 trillion miles (9.5 trillion km) in a year? That's quite another story. And what if,

to make matters worse, we say that the Milky Way Galaxy is over 100,000 light-years across? This would mean that the Milky Way is over 100,000 times 6 trillion miles (9.5 trillion km) across! Can you imagine numbers that large?

Reading about galaxies means reading about time and space — usually huge amounts of time and space. It means numbers so large that it may be impossible to understand exactly what they mean. We can never understand them from anything we do in our day-to-day lives.

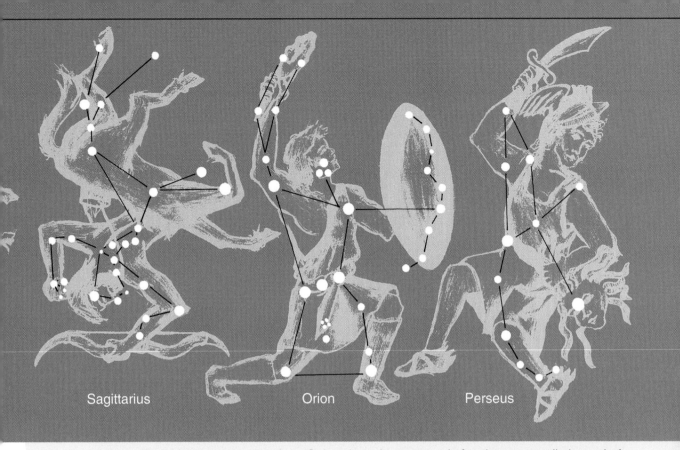

Sagittarius   Orion   Perseus

Above: Four of the spiral arms of our Galaxy have been named after these constellations. *Left to right*, they are Centaurus, the Centaur, half man and half horse; Sagittarius, the Archer; Orion, the Hunter; and Perseus, the hero who killed Medusa, the creature that turned people to stone.

But perhaps we can imagine, if we start with numbers that are small –

• The 18 sheets of paper that make up this book total just over 1/16 inch (about 2 millimeters) in thickness.

• A **million** sheets of paper would be as high as a 32-story building.

• A **billion** sheets of paper would be over 55 miles (90 km) tall — 10 times taller than Mt. Everest!

• A **trillion** sheets would tower more than 59,000 miles (95,000 km) above Earth — more than one-quarter of the way to the Moon!

• If we figure 60 seconds to a minute, and 60 minutes to an hour, then 86,400 seconds make up a 24-hour day.

• A **million** seconds is 12 days.

• A **billion** seconds is more than 31 years.

• A **trillion** seconds adds up to 300 centuries. That's 30,000 years. Thirty thousand years ago, many of our ancestors were still living in caves!

More Books about the Milky Way and Other Galaxies

Astronomy Encyclopedia. Patrick Moore and Leif Robinson (Oxford)

The Birth of Our Universe. Isaac Asimov (Gareth Stevens)

Find the Constellations. H. A. Rey (Houghton Mifflin)

Nebulas. Gregory Vogt (Raintree)

Stars and Galaxies. Robin Kerrod (Raintree)

DVDs

Atlas of the Sky. (Space Holdings)

Stargaze II - Visions of the Universe. (Wea)

Understanding The Universe. (Artisan Entertainment)

Web Sites

The Internet is a good place to get more information about the Milky Way and other galaxies. The web sites listed here can help you learn about the most recent discoveries, as well as those made in the past.

Discovery Channel School.
school.discovery.com/schooladventures/universe/galaxytour/milkyway.html

NASA, Imagine the Universe. imagine.gsfc.nasa.gov/docs/features/objects/milkyway1.html

Students for the Exploration and Development of Space (SEDS).
seds.lpl.arizona.edu/messier/more/mw.html

Windows to the Universe. www.windows.ucar.edu/cgi-bin/tour_def/the_universe/Milkyway.html

Places to Visit

You can explore the Universe without leaving Earth. Here are some museums and centers where you can learn more about our Milky Way and other galaxies.

Adler Planetarium and Astronomy Museum
1300 S. Lake Shore Drive
Chicago, IL 60605-2403

American Museum of Natural History
Rose Center for Earth and Space
Central Park West at 79th Street
New York, NY 10024

Carter Observatory
40 Salamanca Rd
Kelburn
Wellington
New Zealand

Museum of Science, Boston
Science Park
Boston, MA 02114

National Air and Space Museum
Smithsonian Institution
6th and Independence Avenue SW
Washington, DC 20560

Scienceworks Museum
2 Booker Street
Spotswood
Melbourne, Victoria 3015
Australia

Glossary

astronomer: a person involved in the scientific study of the Universe and its various celestial bodies.

barred spiral galaxy: a spiral galaxy in which the arms begin at the ends of a "bar" across the galaxy's center.

binary stars: two stars that circle, or revolve around, each other.

black hole: a tightly packed object with such powerful gravity that not even light can escape from it.

cannibal galaxies: giant galaxies that have collided with and "swallowed" other galaxies.

constellation: a grouping of stars in the sky that seems to trace out a familiar pattern, figure, or symbol.

dark matter: a mysterious substance that seems to be the chief form of matter in the Universe. It does not give off light or other radiation, but can be detected through its gravitational effects.

elliptical: shaped like an oval.

galaxy: a large star system containing up to hundreds of billions of stars, along with gas and dust. Our Galaxy is known as the Milky Way.

globular cluster: a ball-shaped, closely packed grouping of stars. These clusters are commonly found in the outlying parts of a galaxy.

gravity: the force that causes objects like Earth and the Moon to be drawn to one another.

halo: a collection of stars and globular clusters scattered around the disk of a spiral galaxy.

jet: a stream of fast-moving gas or similar material coming from the vicinity of an object such as a star or a black hole.

light-year: the distance that light travels in one year - nearly 6 trillion miles (9.5 trillion km).

Local Group: the small cluster of galaxies to which our Galaxy belongs.

Milky Way: the name of our Galaxy. From Earth's position in the Galaxy, the Milky Way looks like a river of stars in the night sky.

nebula: a cloud of gas and dust in space.

orbit: the path that one celestial object follows as it circles, or revolves around, another.

Orion arm: the spiral arm of our Milky Way Galaxy where our Sun is located.

quasar: an extremely distant object that seems to resemble a star and gives off huge amounts of energy. Quasars seem to be located at the centers of galaxies and involve an enormous black hole.

satellite: an object in space that orbits a larger object.

Solar System: the Sun with the planets and all the other bodies, such as asteroids and comets, that orbit it.

spiral arms: long, curved lines of stars.

spiral galaxy: a type of galaxy that is rather flat and has spiral arms coming from its center. Our Milky Way is a spiral galaxy.

Sun: our star and the provider of the energy that makes life possible on Earth.

supercluster: a collection of clusters of galaxies.

supernova: the explosion of a star during which the star may become a million or more times brighter.

Universe: everything that we know exists and that we believe may exist.

Index

Born in 1920, Isaac Asimov came to the United States as a young boy from his native Russia. As a young man, he was a student of biochemistry. In time, he became one of the most productive writers the world has ever known. His books cover a spectrum of topics, including science, history, language theory, fantasy, and science fiction. His brilliant imagination gained him the respect and admiration of adults and children alike. Sadly, Isaac Asimov died shortly after the publication of the first edition of *Isaac Asimov's Library of the Universe.*

The publishers wish to thank the following for permission to reproduce copyright material: front cover, 3, 8, 17, 20 (lower), 23 (upper), 26 (both), 27, National Optical Astronomy Observatories; 4-5, © Frank Zullo 1985; 6, 7, 11, NASA Goddard Space Flight Center; 9, © Brian Sullivan 1988; 10, © John Foster; 12, 13, © ROE/Anglo-Australian Observatory, David Malin; 14, © Gareth Stevens Inc.; 14-15, 22, NASA; 16 (upper), European Space Agency, NASA, and Jean-Paul Kneib (Observatoire Midi-Pyrénées, France/Caltech, USA); 16 (lower), NASA, ESA, S. Beckwith (STScI), and the HUDF Team; 18, Sheri Gibbs; 19 (upper), © Lynette Cook 1987; 19 (lower), © Sally Bensusen 1987; 20 (upper), European Southern Observatory; 21 (left), Halton C. Arp; 21 (right), Anglo-Australian Telescope Board, David Malin; 23 (lower), NASA and The Hubble Heritage Team (STScI/AURA); 24-25, Holland Ford/NASA; 28-29, © Laurie Shock 1988.